Garfield:
it's a cat-eat-dog world

JIM DAVIS

D0573158

Ballantine Books • New York

Copyright © 1996 by PAWS, Incorporated.

All rights reserved under International and Pan-American Copyright
Conventions. Published in the United States by Ballantine Books, a
division of Random House, Inc., New York, and simultaneously in
Canada by Random House of Canada Limited, Toronto.

http://www.randomhouse.com

Library of Congress Catalog Card Number: 96-95289

ISBN: 0-345-91203-9

Manufactured in the United States of America

First Edition: December 1996

10   9   8   7   6   5   4   3   2

I SUPPOSE I SHOULD LEARN TO LIKE ODIE

BUT I JUST CAN'T RESPECT ANYONE WHO TURNS AROUND THREE TIMES TO LIE DOWN

JIM DAVIS 3-14

PAT PAT PAT PAT

YOU DIDN'T SEE THAT

3-17 JIM DAVIS

© 1979 United Feature Syndicate, Inc.

© 1979 United Feature Syndicate, Inc.

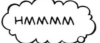

MY AUNT EVELYN IS THE NEATEST CAT I KNOW

© 1979 United Feature Syndicate, Inc. 10-10

SHE PLUCKED ALL THE HAIR OFF HER BODY SO SHE WOULDN'T SHED ON THE FURNITURE

NOW SHE'S LIVING WITH A FAMILY IN L.A. THAT THINKS SHE'S A CHIHUAHUA

JIM DAVIS

YIP!

PUNT!

© 1980 United Feature Syndicate, Inc.

1-9 JIM DAVIS

THE FARM CAT SETS OUT TO PATROL HIS PROPERTY

© 1980 United Feature Syndicate, Inc.

6-12

HE HAPPENS UPON A PLOT OF FRESH CATNIP

AND WAKES UP THE NEXT MORNING IN ATLANTIC CITY WITH A BARBIE DOLL

JIM DAVIS

6-28

© 1980 United Feature Syndicate, Inc.

Z

JIM DAVIS

WHY RIGHT HERE, GARFIELD?

GIMME THAT
HAMBURGER

YOU GET A LOT MORE
ACCOMPLISHED IF YOU
DO IT WITH AUTHORITY

LICK

JIM DAVIS 10-21

© 1982 United Feature Syndicate, Inc.

WHAT HAPPENED TO YOU?

GARFIELD'S LAW:
CATS MOVE AT A SPEED PROPORTIONATE TO THE AMOUNT OF FOOD AT THEIR DESTINATION. THEY MAY EVEN EXCEED THE SPEED OF SOUND

GARFIELD

11-8

JIM DAVIS   © 1982 United Feature Syndicate, Inc.

MEOW

JIM DAVIS 11-7

© 1982 United Feature Syndicate, Inc.

GARFIELD'S LAW: CATS ARE INDEPENDENT. CATS ARE LONERS...

THEY ARE UNDERFOOT ONLY WHEN YOU'RE CARRYING GROCERIES

SORRY ABOUT THAT

GARFIELD'S LAW: CATS INSTINCTIVELY KNOW THE PRECISE MOMENT THEIR OWNERS WILL AWAKE...

THEN THEY AWAKEN THEM TEN MINUTES SOONER

11-10

© 1982 United Feature Syndicate, Inc.

JIM DAVIS

© 1983 United Feature Syndicate, Inc.

AND JUST WHAT DO YOU THINK YOU'RE DOING?

ASSERTING MY CATHOOD?

WHY DO YOU HAVE SUCH LARGE TEETH, GARFIELD?

ALL THE BETTER TO EAT YOU WITH, MY DEAR

STOP THAT!

OBVIOUSLY, SIR, YOU ARE NOT A PATRON OF THE CLASSICS

© 1983 United Feature Syndicate, Inc.

© 1983 United Feature Syndicate, Inc.

7-17 JIM DAVIS

I AM ABOUT TO OUTDO MYSELF

WHAP!

© 1983 United Feature Syndicate, Inc.

WHY IS IT I'M CRAZY ABOUT YOU, GARFIELD?

PROBABLY BECAUSE I'M PERFECT

YOU CLAW THE DRAPES, SHED ON THE FURNITURE, STEAL MY FOOD AND HASSLE THE DOG

© 1983 United Feature Syndicate, Inc.

JIM DAVIS

8·30

NOBODY'S PERFECT

WE ARE NEARING THE BEWITCHING HOUR WHEN EVIL FORCES WELL UP WITHIN ME

I LOVE IT

EEEK!

GARGLE SNORT DROOL

YIP!